Enrich Your Life

World's Classics

100 Greatest Novels of All Time

www.iboo.com

Save
The Ocean
Feed
The World
OCEANA
Restoring the oceans could feed 1 billion people a healty seafood meal each day

10 ON THE COVER

Francois Ntone, living in isolation enabled him to focus on the book he was writing. Finally his book "Grace and Truth: How the Biblical Narrative Affirms that Christ is Supreme and Parts of the Bible Are Obsolete" released in Feb 7, 2021

In this Issue

Page 34 TIPS

**Eight Tips to Prepare
for a Virtual Interview**

With these tips you will be well on your way to not only acing that interview, but job offers galore! Break a leg and most of all, be yourself, and let your personality shine!

PAGE 14

"How COVID-19 Has Changed the Way We Do Business Forever"

PAGE 18

Can a Woman Become More Powerful?
BY REENY CARVOTTA BARRON

PAGE 42

DOES ASTROLOGY REALLY WORK?
BY DHANUSUYA K
If you ask hardened scientists, they will say astrology can't work. On the other hand, believers will give the opposite opinion.

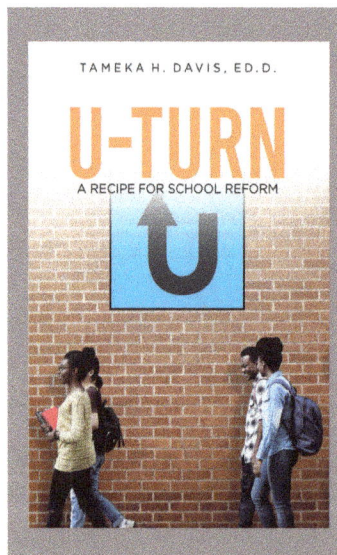

TAMEKA H. DAVIS, ED.D.

U-TURN
A RECIPE FOR SCHOOL REFORM

Page 22 BOOK

Dr. Tameka H. Davis' New Book, 'U-Turn', Leads One in Raising Student Achievers and Building a High Performance Organizational Management

In this Issue

EDITOR'S LETTER

We're so proud to be releasing updated magazine of The Reader's House that exists to connect writers, authors, artists, musicians, coaches who arse always ready to share their story and passion with an interview, and we put them to The Reader's House spotlight. On our cover is acclaimed Author *Francois Ntone*. Like most people, he has been impacted by the pandemic. His wife and he moved to their Florida house and were able to follow the guidance on social distancing fairly easily. On the other hand, living in isolation enabled him to focus on the book he was writing. Finally his book "Grace and Truth: How the Biblical Narrative Affirms that Christ is Supreme and Parts of the Bible Are Obsolete" released in

Feb 7, 2021

We continue to connect people who are always ready to share their story and passion with an interview, and we put them to The Reader's House spotlight. We have interviewed not just acclaimed, as well as award winning authors like *Jennifer Anne Gordon*, a gothic horror/literary fiction novelist, won the Kindle Award for Best Horror/Suspense for 2020, Won Best Horror 2020 from Authors on the Air, was a Finalist for American Book Fest's Best Book Award- Horror, 2020. She also received the Platinum 5 Star Review from Reader's Choice as well as the Gold Seal from Book View.

We featured Enlightened Thought Leader *Dr. Chérie Carter-Scot*t on the cover of March issue. Dr Chérie is #1 New York Times Best Selling Author (19

Books), Oprah Winfrey Endorsed, Consultant to Fortune 500 companies.

International Bestselling Author *Kathrin Hutson*, NY Times Bestseller Author *Tosca Lee*, Acclaimed crime fiction Canadian Author, *Melissa Yi*, Past President of the Sisters In Crime NJ and Award Winning Author, *Kristina Rienzi* are some of authors we will feature on the cover in upcoming issues.

Enjoy Reading

A. Harlowe

The Reader's House

Published by Newyox

LONDON OFFICE
3rd Floor
86-90 Paul Street
London
EC2A 4NE UK

t: +44 20 3828 7097
editor@newyox.com
newyox.com

Due to the current lockdown in England, we are working remotely until further notice. Currently, we are still producing publications; should this change, we will contact any customers this affects. This means our phones have been turned off and we're currently only available by email (editor@newyox.com). We will be answering emails as quickly as possible and we thank you in advance for your patience and understanding. We'll keep our website updated as and when things change.

Editor in Chief
Anna Harlow
Managing Director
Dan Peters
Marketing Director
Ben Alan

CONTRIBUTORS

Mickey Mikkelson
Rian Donatelli

Reeny Carvotta Barron
Lisa Brown Gilbert
Andy Machin
Rocky Cole
Jean Taylor
Rosina S Khan
BY Dhanusuya K
Anders Abadie
Vinod Vullikanti
Hannah Spraker
We assume no responsibility for unsolicited manuscripts or art materials.

FRANCOIS NTONE

Presents the past, reveals the present, and creates the future

Currently, in the United States, evangelicals are under scrutiny because of their behavior and their adherence to "Christian nationalist" views.

BY DAN PETERS
May 6, 2021

Tell us about yourself and your work.

I am, by profession, an engineer who recently retired after a 33-year career. I earned a PhD degree in Mechanical Engineering from Clemson University, with a specialty in Computational Fluid Dynamics (CFD), a field of knowledge that was a novelty at the time. I subsequently joined Cummins, Inc., a fortune 500 company that manufactures internal combustion engines and associated components for use in trucks and other industrial applications. At Cummins, I pioneered the use of CFD as a means of providing insights, through computer simulations, into the various processes associated with fluid flow in an engine.

Before the introduction of computer simulations, engine components were designed and developed using experimental testing: numerous variations of a part were fabricated and tested at a substantial cost, and the ones yielding the best performance were selected for production. With the availability of increasingly powerful computers and the development of mathematical models to simulate increasingly complex physical phenomena, it became possible to analyze the performance of parts before actually making them. Such a capability offered the potential to considerably reduce development costs, but while some of the physical processes involved could be handled effectively early on, others were extremely complex and required sustained research in collaboration with universities and government agencies.

I became a company leader in these efforts, and over time, my team demon

Continued *on page 16*

I am also currently writing a book that refutes ideas promoted on this matter by John Calvin, one of the influential theologians of the Reformation."
FRANCOIS NTONE

It's time to take a stand for homeless pets. It's time to adopt change. Every day, more than 4,100 dogs and cats are killed in shelters across the country — but **with Best Friends Animal Society leading the way, and your support, we can help our nation's shelters and Save Them All**

SAVE
THEM
ALL

"HOW COVID-19 Has Changed the Way We Do Business FOREVER"

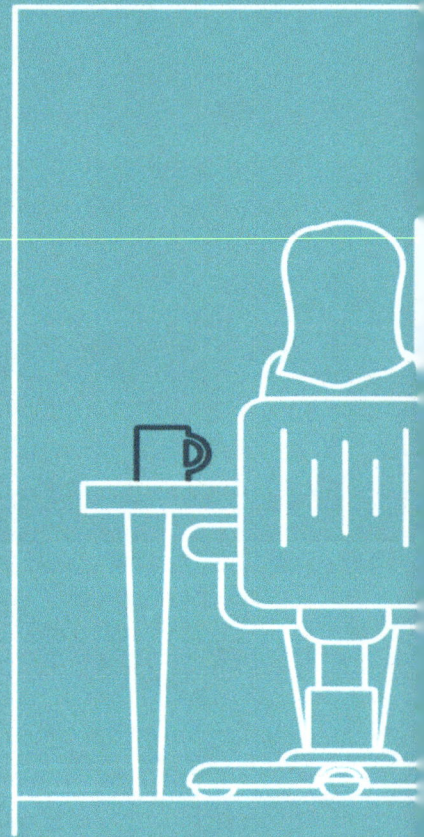

Most executives surveyed wish that they'd invested even more in technology over the past 12 months.

"When investments are imperative, borrowing or leasing may be the right solution to acquiring the technology needed to remain competitive."

survey.

Conducted by The Harris Poll for CIT Group Inc., a leading national bank focused on empowering businesses and personal savers, the survey of leaders of U.S. middle-market and small businesses is designed to illuminate the intersection of technology and talent. Compared to last year's survey, significantly more leaders today believe continuous technological investment is a business requirement.

"The resiliency and flexibility that technology can deliver businesses has been convincingly proven by COVID-19," says David Harnisch, president of CIT's Commercial Finance division. "Business leaders have taken that lesson to heart and are focused on making technology a fundamental part of their 'tomorrow thinking'."

Most executives surveyed wish that they'd invested even more in technology over the past 12 months. In fact, more than three in four middle market executives believe investments in technology would have helped their company fare better during the pandemic. For small businesses, roughly half felt similarly.

However, there's little question how important technology will be going forward, with the majority of respondents saying it's crucial to future success.

Seemingly determined not to repeat the mistake of under-investing, the majority plan to invest as much or more in their business over the next 12 months as compared to the past year. Only 15% of small businesses say they may invest less this coming year, likely due to financial constraints resulting from the pandemic.

"Small businesses don't always have the financial resources that larger enterprises often enjoy,"

says Ken Martin, managing director of CIT's Small Business Solutions group. "When investments are imperative, borrowing or leasing may be the right solution to acquiring the technology needed to remain competitive." When it comes to these upgrades, investments that make it easier for employees to work remotely are a clear priority. Over the next 12 months, 71% of middle market executives and 31% of small business leaders who plan to invest will spend on technology that facilitates remote work.

"It's not just a matter of convenience. Businesses that empower employees to work remotely have a clear competitive advantage," says Denise Menelly, CIT's executive vice president and head of Technology and Operations.

This is a trend that's likely here to stay. Approximately a quarter of small businesses operating remotely expect -- and want -- these changes to remain permanent after COVID-19 subsides, and about 40% of middle market executives expect the same, with some seeing it as a means to grow the company.

However, this digital transformation puts a premium on a tech-savvy workforce able to support customers and collaborate with colleagues remotely. While many believe their current workforce has the skills to keep up, businesses are also substantially more likely than last year to say companies need to focus on hiring tech-savvy talent.

While the COVID-19 pandemic has created a great deal of uncertainty for small and midsized businesses, it has in many ways clarified what's needed to remain successful in an evolving world.

(StatePoint)

The COVID-19 pandemic has fundamentally changed how business gets done. And when it comes to midsized and small businesses, the importance of investing in new technology, facilitating remote work and maintaining a tech-savvy workforce has never been so clear, according to a new

← **Continued** *from page 11*

strated the ability not only to help solve perennial product problems that had cost the company millions of dollars in warranty, but also to help develop new, more reliable products faster and at a lower cost. The company adopted a new philosophy called Analysis-Led Design, to be applied to the entire product development process. To help with its implementation, in 2004, I spent 6 months in India where I contributed to the creation of a research center focusing on computer simulation. In 2009, I was a recipient of the company's prestigious Julius

Truth: How the Biblical Narrative Affirms that Christ Is Supreme and Parts of the Bible Are Obsolete.

Is the kingdom of God not in heaven?

In the Bible, Jesus focuses on the kingdom of God as a way of life on earth which is consistent with God's will. Even though it has promises for the afterlife, it puts a great deal of emphasis on human conduct on earth, which must be guided by the ideas of love, peace, justice and forgiveness. These ideas are a reflection of God's true nature.

Does Christianity not live up to those expectations?

the lead in supporting wars abroad, and they oppose efforts to help the poor and the disadvantaged. The attack on the U.S. Capitol by insurrectionists, which occurred on January 6, was recognized as the work of Christian nationalists by thoughtful Christian leaders who were quick to denounce it and distance themselves from it.

How can your book help with this situation?

There is, currently, a renewed awareness that a Christian must be "Christ-like," and there are books being written on that. But many Christians also believe that the Bible is God's Inerrant Word, and that does not necessarily lead to "Christ-centered" beliefs. Indeed, the biblical narrative, which is lengthy and intricate, presents theological and ethical beliefs that change in time. Unfortunately, influential Christians often attempt to harmonize all aspects of the Bible, thereby creating the false impression that all pronouncements in it are equally divine and relevant. The assumption that the Old Testament and the New Testament are equal is very common among conservative Christians. If it is true, then they can go back and forth between the two testaments and select statements that support their own agenda.

But that amounts to a rewriting of the Bible. As an example, I explain in my book that the book of Exodus presents Moses, the Israelite lawgiver, as a student of the divine rather than God's mouthpiece. Moses encounters an unknown God at Horeb, and struggles to understand him for the rest of his life. In fact, the revelation he receives about God's compassionate nature comes to him at a time he is seeking divine guidance, well after he has presented the Ten Commandments to his people. At that time, he is also told that he will never grasp the fullness of God's nature. This has to be contrasted with the declaration in the New Testament that those who have seen Christ have seen God (John 14:9). The title of my book, Grace and Truth, comes from a succinct statement of that evolution: "For the law was given through Moses; grace and truth came through Jesus Christ. No one has ever seen God, but the one and only Son, who is himself

> *In the Bible, Jesus focuses on the kingdom of God as a way of life on earth which is consistent with God's will. Even though it has promises for the afterlife, it puts a great deal of emphasis on human conduct on earth, which must be guided by the ideas of love, peace, justice and forgiveness. These ideas are a reflection of God's true nature.*

Perr Award on innovation for my contributions to the combustion system development process. In 2020, at the time I retired, I received a national award, the Black Engineer of the Year Award, in the Principal Investigator category.

My professional background, which is highly analytical, has also been useful to me in an area I have been strongly interested in: religious studies. I grew up as a Christian and I have been involved in Church leadership activities for three decades, including teaching about the Bible. I am aware of the positive contributions made by Christianity throughout its history. I am also aware of its shortcomings, and particularly its ethical failures. As a Bible study teacher, I know that many Christians do not have a good understanding of the flow of ideas in the Bible, as related to matters of theology and ethics. In fact, there is a serious gap between churchgoers and Bible scholars in that respect. Many Christians still believe that God himself wrote the Bible and that the kingdom of God, Jesus' primary emphasis, is in heaven. In order to help reduce the gap, I wrote and published a book titled Grace and

There is no doubt that overall, Christianity has had a positive impact on human history in that regard. However, it has also condoned violence, wars, social inequalities, witch hunts, inquisitions. In some cases, it has even been an obstacle to intellectual progress.

Today, some Christian leaders seem surprised that many churchgoers are far from projecting the "salt of the world" image envisioned by Jesus. Currently, in the United States, evangelicals are under scrutiny because of their behavior and their adherence to "Christian nationalist" views. In a 2017 article, the editor-in-chief of Christianity Today, an evangelical Christian, asked the question: "What is wrong with these evangelicals? Who's teaching them these unmerciful attitudes?" This is because evangelicals lead the way in opposing efforts towards diversity and are driven by strong tribal attitudes. They oppose efforts towards gun control and do not seem to care about gun violence. They support political candidates with questionable morals who promise to restore to them political and economic privileges they think they lost. They take

God and is in closest relationship with the Father, has made him known." (John 1:17-18)

There are implications associated with only having partial knowledge of God's character. Bible readers will notice that Moses gives many commands that do not reflect God's love and compassion as seen in Christ. Therefore, Christians who understand that, in the final analysis, Christ is the one who really matters, will no longer turn to ideas in the Law of Moses that are inconsistent with the teaching of Jesus. My book is the result of an effort to rigorously track theological and ethical changes throughout the Bible, to help Christians and other Bible readers understand the full story which, in the end, is about the supremacy of Christ. From that perspective, ideas of universal love replace the notion of a chosen nation that must separate itself from

conservative church was short-lived and left me very disappointed, with the feeling that the church leaders were trying to feed me a narrative inconsistent with my own reading of the Bible. I later joined a congregation with a worldview closer to mine. I became a member of the Church Council and was even made chairman of the Mutual Ministry Committee, which was in charge of supporting the staff and deal with conflicts. At that time, I participated in various Bible studies and became a teacher. I also began to seriously study scholarly material on Bible-related topics. My studies confirmed views that I already had, while also broadening my knowledge of historical, theological and ethical aspects of Christianity.

As a Sunday School teacher, I began to raise an awareness among fellow Christians on the fact that the teach-

easily. However, we lived in isolation, and that takes a toll after a while. In particular, the inability to directly participate in church activities has been an unwelcome change.

On the other hand, living in isolation enabled me to focus on the book I was writing. I published it myself and, in addition to finalizing the manuscript, I had to learn many aspects of ebook publishing to complete the project. I had plenty of time to do that. I was also able to spend more time on maintaining my website.

How do you advertise your book?

This is an area to which I am currently directing my efforts. My website, k-of-g.com, has been in existence for some time and is my starting point. I am issuing press releases, and I am pursuing opportunities to introduce the book contents to the public through direct interactions with audiences and through mass media. It is work in progress.

> My interest in the Bible was renewed after my mother passed away. I was 32 years old at that time, and I was looking for answers to questions about the meaning of life and life after death. My brief experience with a very conservative church was short-lived and left me very disappointed, with the feeling that the church leaders were trying to feed me a narrative inconsistent with my own reading of the Bible.

others. God is no longer a Warrior-God, but one whose true children are peacemakers. Wealth is no longer a divine reward for righteousness, but a distraction to those who seek the kingdom of God. Sickness is no longer punishment for sin, etc.

How did you get started in this endeavor, which is a departure from your professional background?

I was raised by Christian parents. During my college years, I did not attend church services regularly, even though I still had reverence for the person of Christ. My interest in the Bible was renewed after my mother passed away. I was 32 years old at that time, and I was looking for answers to questions about the meaning of life and life after death. My brief experience with a very

ing material commonly used made assumptions that led to inappropriate conclusions. I was dealing with open-minded Christians, and I was successful in changing their perspectives simply because I could show them, in a rigorous manner, what the Bible really says, especially in passages that are not commonly discussed in Bible studies or Sunday sermons. My book is a result of decades of reflection on such matters.

Have you been impacted by the Covid-19 Pandemic?

Like most people, I have been impacted by the pandemic. I was fortunate that it started right after my retirement. My wife and I moved to our Florida house and were able to follow the guidance on social distancing fairly

To what do you attribute what you have achieved so far?

I think it is fair to say that my involvement in teaching about the Bible has been driven by my passion for it. Also, as I look at the constant turmoil in the world, I strongly believe that Christ remains the best hope for humanity. For that reason, I have dedicated a great deal of my time to studying, teaching and writing. My professional background helps me in my endeavor because I am trained to sort out complex sets of data and draw meaningful conclusions from them.

What are your goals for the near future?

My main goal is to do what I can to promote the idea that Christians should focus on the teaching of Christ and not return to the parts of the Old Testament that conflict with it. I am also currently writing a book that refutes ideas promoted on this matter by John Calvin, one of the influential theologians of the Reformation. ●

Can a Woman Become More Powerful?

Can a Woman be more powerful and stand out in her own feminine energy and take a stand?

As a woman, avoiding conflict to stay in peace is like: the nurturing mother of a child

BY REENY CARVOTTA BARRON

a partner of passion

a flower of sweetness.

But, we deny ourselves

• Inability to be in the present moment.
• Doubt (inability to trust our abilities - always need to be perfect)
• Impatience (the stubbornness to refuse the present until a certain outcome is

Can a Woman be more powerful and stand out in her own feminine energy and take a stand?
As a woman, avoiding conflict to stay in peace is like:
the nurturing mother of a child
a partner of passion
a flower of sweetness.

achieved)
• Projection of negative beliefs, values and ideals permeating onto the universe.
• Closing our minds to possibilities that surpass our wildest dreams.
• The need to control by setting limits that make us comfortable and forsake the big picture, such as time limits, physical attributes, moral imperatives, etc.
• An unwillingness to allow through surrender

Let's Start with Surrender

Our beliefs hold us strong. Everything in ur lives can be embraced. Everything in life is a l esson and our reactions can create or deny opportunity. S urrendering to actually being vulnerable takes courage.

a flower of sweetness

We all have a strong internal compass that keeps us focused inward keeping use safe from our perceptions of reality.

• Intention (the will to confidently assert your vision)
• Surrender (Let Go, Let God) no investment in how your dream manifests
• Detachment from the outcome (seeking no outward expression of the item.)
• Flexibility (all while still 'knowing')

• By surrendering judgment, you allow others complete autonomy because you are offering radical acceptance.

Of others: By allowing others to be who they are, you allow yourself to be who you are. It is impossible to be in alignment if you are passing judgement on others. Our lives carry our energy and when we are wanting a particular outcome, our feeling can leave us disconnected from what is true.

Surrender judgment

Of situations: by surrendering judgment of circumstances, we insert ourselves directly into the flow of what is. This is the space acceptance without judgments and fears clearing the error thoughts that block our feminine power.

Courage

Courage breeds success, but how do you build the confidence?

You build it by building your personal resources.

Stretch beyond your comfort zone.

Whether it's through personal development, spiritual practice, coaching, all of the above or anything else that helps you be more of who you are.

Doing something you've never done before and finding you can do it.

Even it you are not equipped, build the courage to have the confidence. Being vulnerable

Stepping out of your EGO it tough. Our ego likes to keep us safe creating illusions of danger. With courage comes an inner strength and confidence - will breed success.

BE THAT PERSON WHO DESIR

Stretch beyond your confort zone

WOMAN

Check out those disarming beliefs harboring your from stepping out. Are they real? Are they quantified?

Even with all the actions you put into place without courage and the ability to surrender we sabotage our self worth. Imagine: a little wall flower full of potential expecting to be rescued.

It can be an uphill battle(!) Free what is inside of you and step beyond. Life is too short to waste on unnecessary logic. Rewrite your reality and give yourself a reason to change.

Do dare to dream bigger dreams. Trust in the wisdom and the gifts that created you. Whatever direction it may take you-you will have the courage to travel beyond.

When the twilight of your life arrives, as it surely will, it will matter not whether you managed to achieve your vision, but that you had the courage to surrender and pursue it.

Reeny coaches individuals who are stuck, afraid, unsure, in transition, struggling with self-doubt, frustration, falling back to old patterns

As a Soul Purpose Coach, she uses techniques to awaken your heart and open your intuitive powers guiding individuals to embrace a soul aligned path to life that will bring greater joy, freedom, success, and inner peace.

Her blogs, includes inspirational articles are written for those who are seeking a new view to looking at life.

Get access to her new book 'The Art of Feminine Power' https://purpose-passionandpossibilities.com

IN LIFE AND BUSINESS - SWEEPING ACTIONS WITHOUT COMPROMISE!

Dr. Tameka H. Davis' New Book,

'U-Turn', Leads One in Raising Student Achievers and Building a High Performance Organizational Management

VICKSBURG, Miss., May 24, 2021 (Newswire.com) - Fulton Books author Tameka H. Davis, Ed.D., a dynamic educational leader, has completed her most recent book "U-Turn": a useful read for leaders to gain wisdom and knowledge in fostering a school for the better. Containing proven effective practices and teaching methods, one will soon witness the institution be filled with success and empowered students and educators.

Tameka writes, "Have you experienced educational burnout? Tired of burning the midnight oil strategizing on how to bring about change within your organization? Are you tired of holes being drilled in the boat while trying to reach your destination? Let's make a U-turn to change the direction of your organization toward success. U-Turn: A Recipe for School Reform equips educational leaders with the tools necessary to make a profound and lasting difference in the lives of students growing up in poverty by changing the culture of their learning environment and making learning relevant to their everyday lives. Dr. Tameka H. Davis transforms an elementary and high school that were classified as high-poverty schools into high-performing schools. In both organizations, Dr. Davis changed the ethos and culture, provided high-performance organizational management, high-quality aligned instructional systems, recruited and cultivated high-quality teachers and teaching, and led with equity ensuring that all students had access to opportunities and resources.

"Readers should expect to:

• Understand the urgency of poverty and how the learning environment has a direct impact on their academic achievement.

• Understand the importance of building authentic student relationships.

TAMEKA H. DAVIS, ED.D.

U-TURN
A RECIPE FOR SCHOOL REFORM

• Understand the importance of building the confidence of students.

• Understand the power of allowing students to have ownership of their data.

• Understand the rationale behind setting goals that are attainable for students."

Published by Fulton Books, Dr. Tameka H. Davis' book is a brilliant key into moving forward and making an impact in today's educational climate.

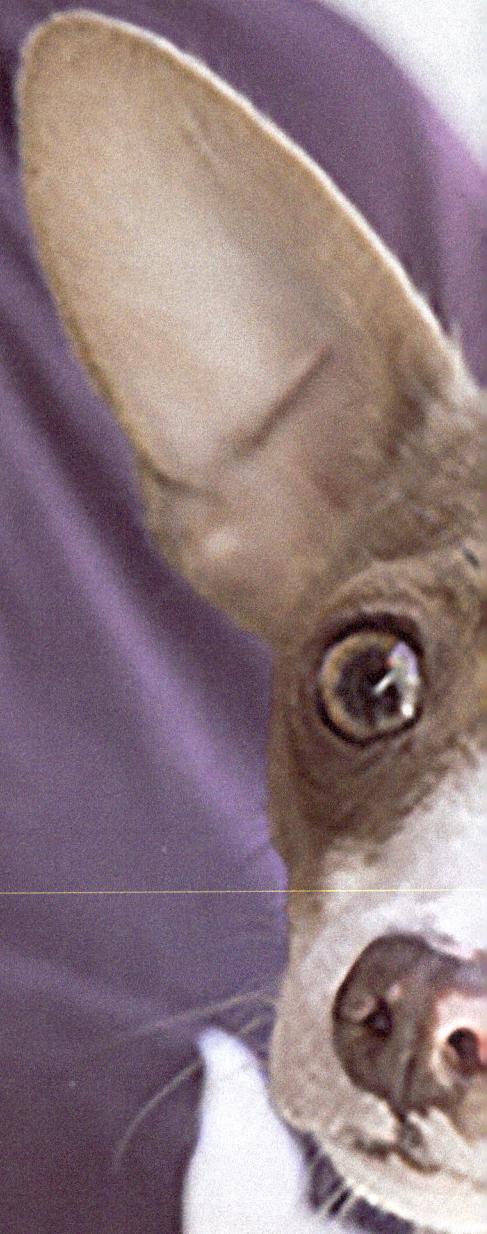

WE WILL NOT TAKE THIS SITTING DOWN

It's time to take a stand for homeless pets. It's time to adopt change. Every day, more than 4,100 dogs and cats are killed in shelters across the country — but **with Best Friends Animal Society leading the way, and your support, we can help our nation's shelters and Save Them All**

SAVE
THEM
ALL

TIPS FROM A DOCTOR
Who Survived COVID-19

TAKE CARE OF YOUR MENTAL HEALTH. COVID-19 IS ISOLATING AND CAN CAUSE DEPRESSION AND ANXIETY.

No matter how strictly you follow the rules, those with firsthand experience know that anyone can get COVID-19.

"Given my role helping shape COVID-19 policies and procedures since the pandemic surfaced, I know the rules better than most: wear a mask, limit social gatherings, stay six feet apart and so on," says Dr. Gina Conflitti, chief medical officer for Medicare products at Cigna, one of the nation's largest health care insurers. "Like many others, I did my best to follow the safety guidance. Yet, in late November 2020, I contracted the virus and faced months of recovery." While Dr. Conflitti hopes this doesn't happen to others, she offers the following advice to those who do contract COVID-19:

• COVID-19 impacts everyone differently. There are those who cruise through COVID-19 with no symptoms while others have mild symptoms. Some people literally fight for their lives. Don't expect to have the same experience as others, and be sure to communicate with your doctor about the best treatment approach.

• Don't get caught in the blame game. Once you contract COVID-19, there's a tendency to blame yourself. Or you might blame others for infecting you. Many never find out how they were exposed. While contact tracing is important, don't waste time blaming yourself or others. Save your energy for recovery.

• Don't be afraid to ask for help. COVID-19 is humbling, and even active, independent people may suddenly need help with normal daily activities, like getting groceries and medicines. People want to help, so don't hesitate to ask so you can concentrate on recovering.

• Take care of your mental health. COVID-19 is

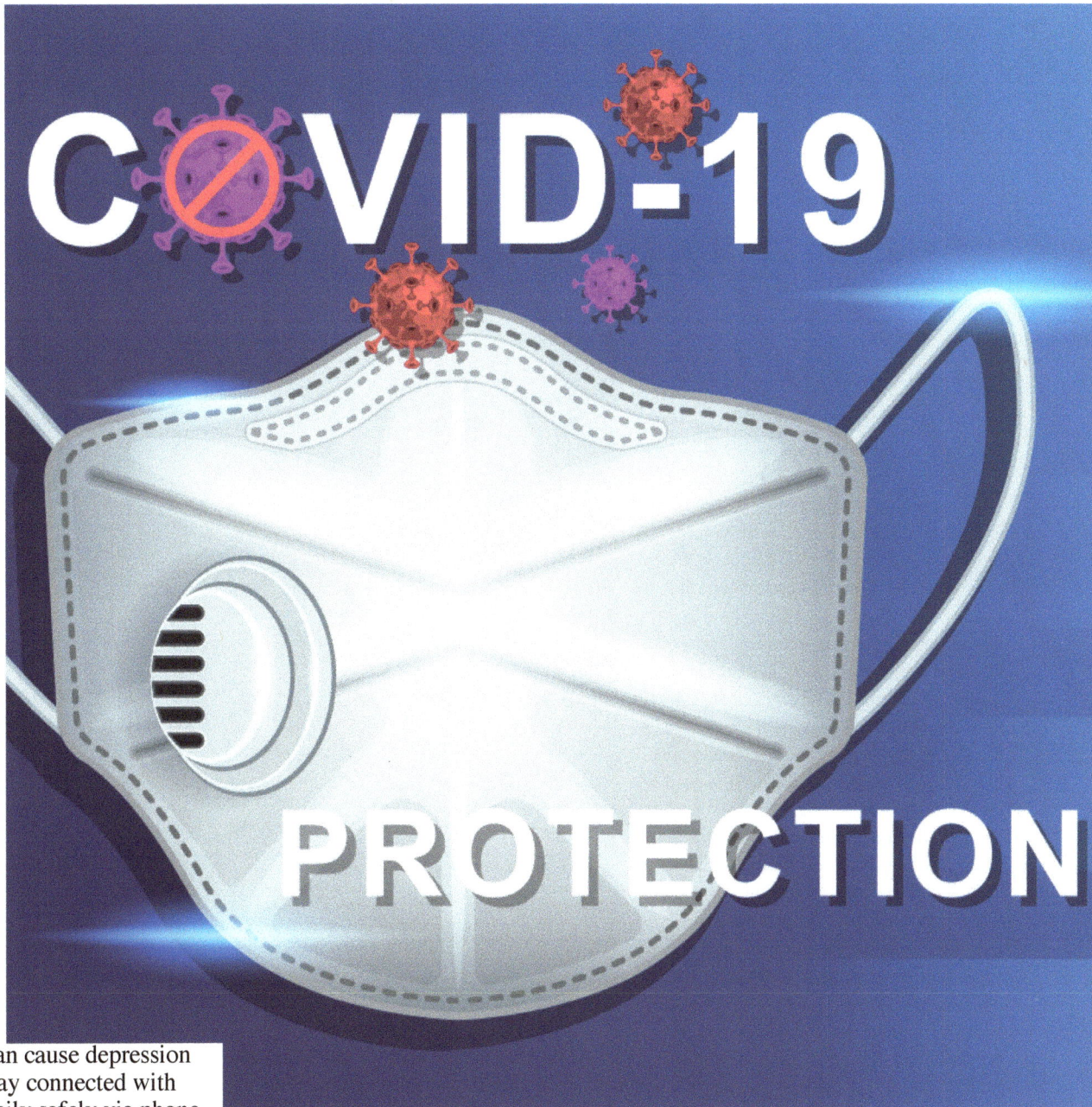

COVID-19 PROTECTION

isolating and can cause depression and anxiety. Stay connected with friends and family safely via phone or video calls. Talk to a professional if things become too difficult to manage on your own. You may have access to behavioral health support through your medical insurance or Medicare plan.

• Listen to your body. There's no good time to get sick. Nevertheless, it's important to listen to your body before returning to work, school and daily activities. Don't rush it. Prepare by eating healthy, getting enough sleep, drinking plenty of water, taking vitamins or supplements if your doctor recommends and reducing stress.

• Pay it forward. Even with all the bad things COVID-19 brings, it's also revealed some of the best

Your Your

aspects of humanity. Pay kindness forward by showing gratitude to clinicians, teachers, restaurant and grocery store workers and others who courageously give their best so our lives are better during this pandemic.

• Get the vaccine. Take control of your health by getting vaccinated. Follow your local health department news, and get your COVID-19 vaccination as soon as medically approved. It's available at no cost and

critical to ensuring your safety and the safety of others.

For Cigna's COVID-19 resources, visit cigna.com/coronavirus.

"It's been a difficult time for all of us, but I'm confident the most challenging days are behind us. Stay safe, follow safety procedures and get vaccinated. The only way we can move forward is if we do it together," says Dr. Conflitti.

BOOK REVIEW

Dancing With Death

BY LISA BROWN GILBERT

Offering an intensely evocative and aptly titled narrative, Dancing with Death both guides and inspires, armchair adventurers as well as venturesome travelers to the jungles, seas, people and cultures of the world's "roads" less traveled within the beautiful panoramas of Latin America. Co-authored by co-adventurers Jean-Philippe Soulé and Luke Shullenberger, this dynamic read memorializes not only their experiences during their expansive sea kayaking journey, but also serves to help bring awareness to the cultures and history of the seldom seen or noted native peoples they encountered.

From the start, the story treats the mind to the emotions and visages entwined in this thrilling narrative which memorializes the unforgettable and awe-inspiring expedition by sea touted as a one of a kind undertaking. Author, guide, and adventurer Jean-Philippe Soulé accompanied by fellow adventurer and able friend Luke Shullenberger find themselves and their kayaks sorely tested by weather, tides and their bodies as they paddled thousands of miles braving often life-threatening conditions including near drowning, malaria, shark attacks, crocodiles, guerrillas, armed bandits and corruption during their one of a kind undertaking. The overall journey spanning three years, 3000 miles and seven countries included Baja, Belize, Guatemala, Honduras, Nicaragua, Costa Rica, and Panama. The expedition fully titled as the Central America Sea Kayaking Expedition 2000, but also known as the CASKE2000, was a quest intended as an effort to connect with, learn about and preserve in writing the history of the self-reliant, indigenous peoples and their respect for and relationship with the earth. Overall, the book provides an absorbing view of life for the two sea bound

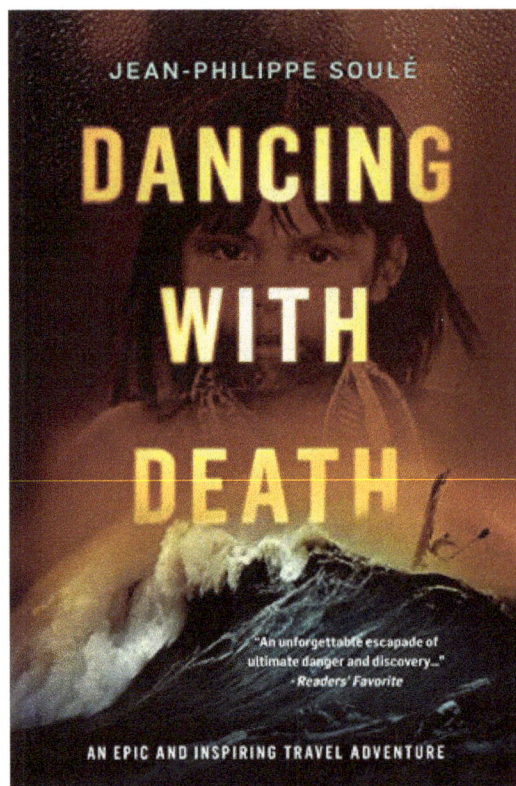

JEAN-PHILIPPE SOULÉ

DANCING WITH DEATH

"An unforgettable escapade of ultimate danger and discovery..."
- *Readers' Favorite*

AN EPIC AND INSPIRING TRAVEL ADVENTURE

ABOUT JEAN-PHILIPPE SOULÉ
"Jean-Philippe's life is like the ultimate ultra-marathon, where hope, perseverance, and grit determine the outcome."
-- Dean Karnazes, ultramarathoner and NY Times bestselling author
Now known for his photographic work for National Geographic and the United Nations, Jean-Philippe Soulé spent his childhood in the beautiful outdoors pushing physical boundaries.
He joined the French Special Forces elite mountain commandos in 1985. Later, driven by a desire for adventure and his passion for meeting diverse people, Jean-Philippe left his native France to travel the world. This quest morphed him from a starry-eyed child to a recognized explorer, but only at the cost of abandoning the conditioning of the modern world and daring to do the impossible: a lesson he hopes encourages other dreamers who refuse to listen when told "they can't."

kayakers. Readers are made privy to the challenges, successes, and failures of their journey supplied via their intimate thoughts and experiences through the inclusion of their alternating journal entries, of which I found did well to enhance the read by providing deep insight and focus to emotions with differing perspectives concerning the elements of planning, preparation, and embarking on the expedition.

Altogether, I did enjoy reading Dancing with Death. The book was easy to engage with and well-organized. I found the narrative an intelligently composed chronicle and compelling read that riled the senses with descriptive exposition and well-organized literate visions of superhuman determination, extreme traveling adventure, fraught with kayaking adventure, spine-tingling moments, exotic environments and intriguing people and cultures.

I also enjoyed their close up encounters with wildlife which maade for particularly exciting reading especially the section on playing hide and seek with giant sea turtles. Additionally, aside from portraying a phenomenal travel super-adventure, included in the book are some of the most stunning photos that I have seen, as well as the additional perk of a fantastically organized website where you get to experience even more details of their journey. However, the very best aspect of the book is the inspirational tone of the whole book. The authors, although faced with the adversity and danger of their expedition, did not quit. They simply followed their dreams, a must I think, for all travelers. I definitely and heartily recommend this for fans of travel books.
Source: EzineArticles

With metrics for COVID-19 improving, many companies are starting to consider returning to work in person. But most employees and employers agree it won't look like it did before.

Indeed, research shows a large chunk of companies today are sizing their physical offices down, as more people work from home all the time or part of the week. And hybrid offices, arrangements where team members are in two or three days a week and work remotely the rest of the time, seem to be the wave of the future.

However, experts say that business owners and managers should not approach hybrid offices the same way they do completely remote set-ups.

"While there are very specific benefits to hybrid offices, they come with their own set of challenges," says Michele Havner, director of marketing at Eturi, the maker of Motiv, a recently-introduced app that small- and mid-sized business owners are using to improve productivity.

Motiv is a mobile dashboard that delivers important productivity metrics to CEOs, managers and leaders. The tool's reporting focuses on providing conference call activity and email summaries and integrates with Google Workspace and Microsoft 365, with many additional integrations and features slated for future release. Havner says that such tools function as a virtual corner office vantage point, helping to smooth out communication, collaboration and workflow issues created by hybrid arrangements and decentralized workspaces.

Equally important to communication is simply being mindful that hybrid offices can cause challenging dynamics among team members. Taking steps to address those issues preemptively can save headaches down the line. This includes making everyone accountable for meeting goals and deadlines. It might also mean offering the same perks to in-office and work-from-home staffers, while giving those who come into a centralized workspace the same level of flexibility remote work affords.

Easily adopted by small- and medium-sized businesses, which have been underserved by existing productivity solutions, Motiv is available through the iOS App Store and Google Play Store. To learn more, visit motivapp.com.

While hybrid offices can ultimately reduce costs and help keep employees healthy and safe, business owners will need to stay flexible and keep their workforce focused. Leveraging tools that facilitate hybrid work situations will be a key to success for companies as they move forward.

HOW TO MAKE A HYBRID WORK-FORCE SUCCESSFUL

PHOTO BY DRAZEN ZIGIC / ISTOCK VIA GETTY IMAGES PLUS

INDEED, RESEARCH SHOWS A LARGE CHUNK OF COMPANIES TODAY ARE SIZING THEIR PHYSICAL OFFICES DOWN, AS MORE PEOPLE WORK FROM HOME ALL THE TIME OR PART OF THE WEEK.

StatePoint

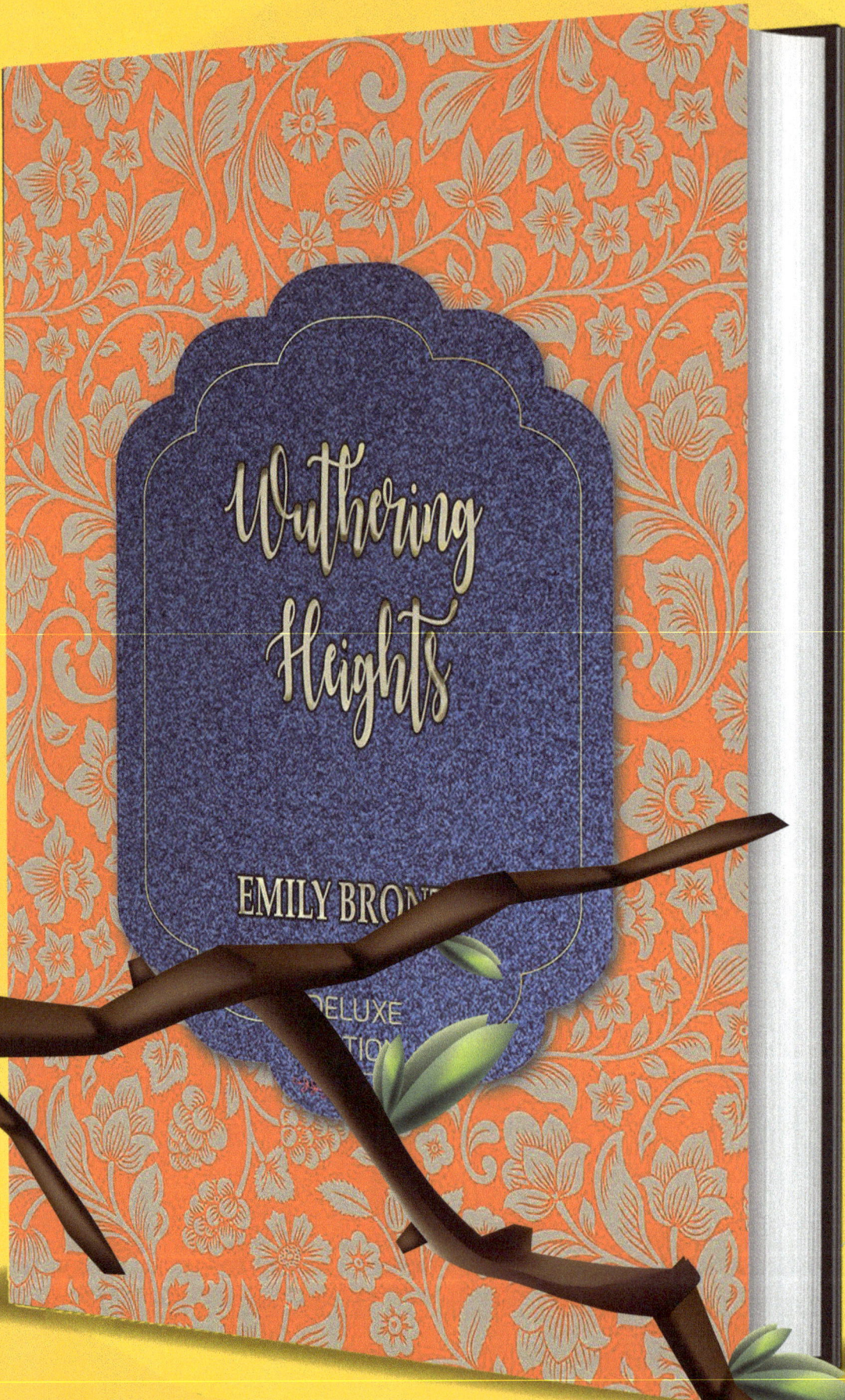

Wuthering Heights

EMILY BRONTË

DELUXE EDITION

Deluxe Edition

Collected from the Guardiand's and
the Telegraph's "the 100 greatest novels of all time" list.

Preserved the original format whilst repairing
imperfections present in the aged copy.

See the complete list at
iboo.com

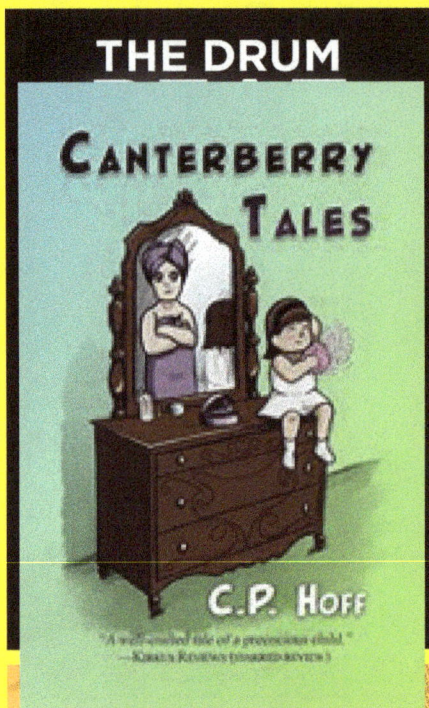

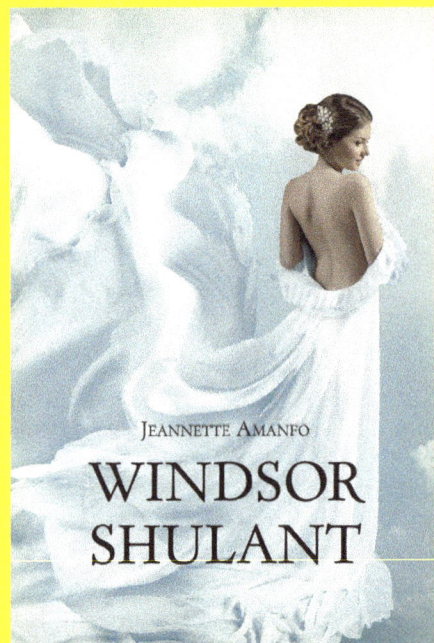

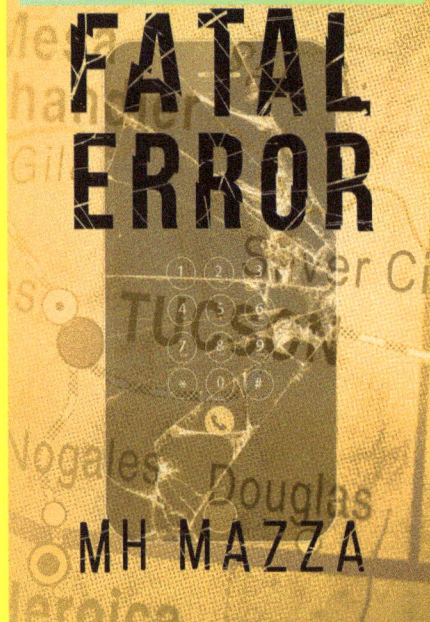

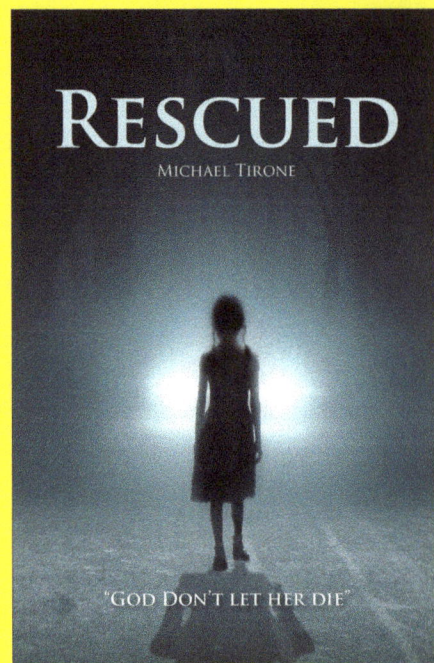

New

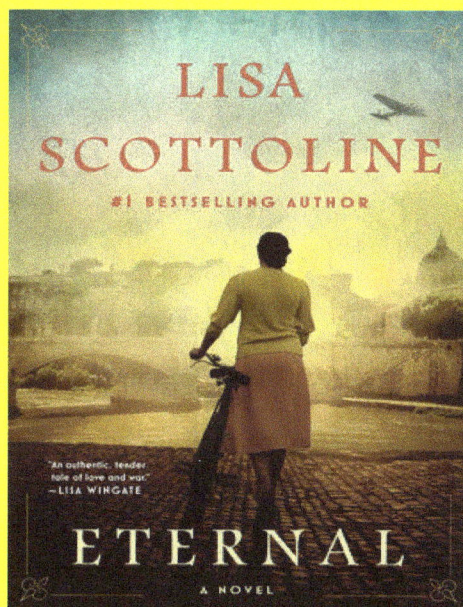

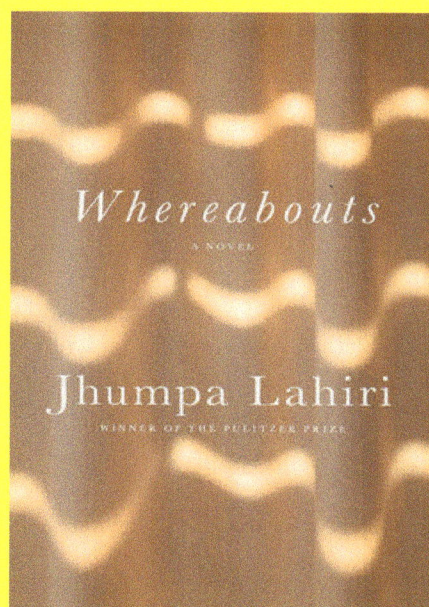

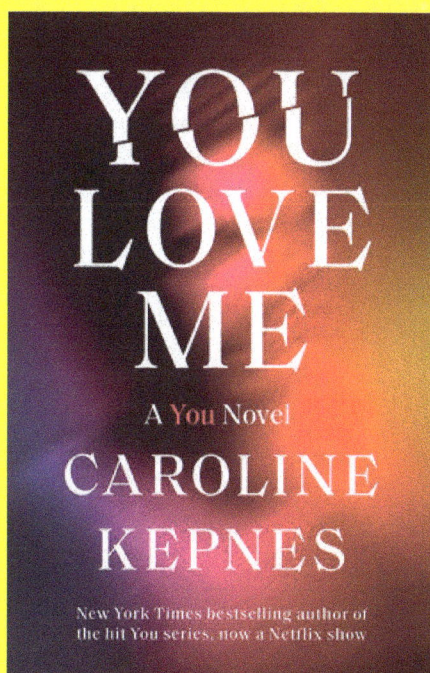

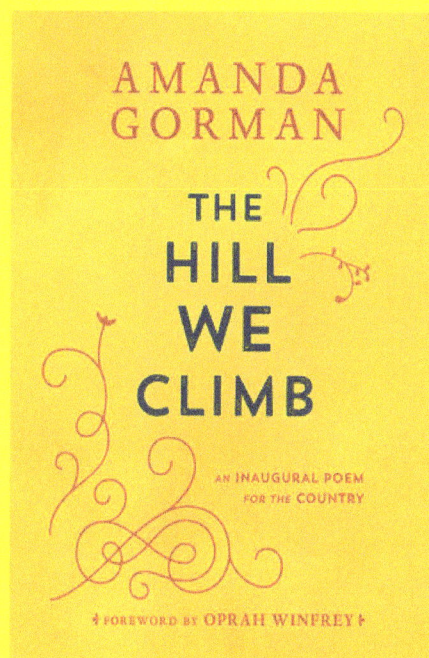

Small Business

8

TIPS

Eight Tips to Prepare
FOR A VIRTUAL INTERVIEW

With these tips you will be well on your way to not only acing that interview, but job offers galore! Break a leg and most of all, be yourself, and let your personality shine!

BY RIAN DONATELLI

First and foremost, it is still a "real" interview, and should be treated as such. There is a person on the other end who will be making an executive decision about your qualifications for the job, so assume it's no different than if you met this individual in person.

Dress to impress! Even if they won't see your feet, dressing from head to toe in at least business casual attire is the first way to not only look professional when the camera goes live, but help you get into the right mindset. You'll be surprised how you will feel you can take on the world when you LOOK like you can!

Find a quiet and professional location for the interview. If you have a home office, this is perfect. If not, most libraries offer conference rooms free of charge, which you can reserve for yourself for the duration of the interview. There is nothing less

professional than children, pets, or other household distractions infringing on your interview experience, and greatly affecting your appearance of professionalism. If you cannot get away from the home, set up at a dining room table or in a living room, and make sure everyone in the home knows you need some privacy for the allotted amount of time.

Try out the interview system in question before the interview. The day or night before, log on and familiarize yourself if it's a program you've never used. Even if it is something you use often, like Face-Time, double check that you have the contact info correct.

Pay close attention to the time zone the interviews are conducted in. This one is SO important. With the advent of virtual interviews, corporations have opened themselves up to a huge network of individuals all over the world, and while advantageous, also likely means they operate on a different time zone than yourself. No one wants to get off on a bad foot because you missed your interview or were late because you were unsure of the time zone. If it isn't clarified anywhere in a confirmation of any kind, reach out to your recruiter or interviewer, they will be happy to give you the information, and glad that you were proactive.

Try to use a laptop or desktop if at all possible, but if you have to use a Smartphone, set up a tripod system beforehand, so your hands can be free for the interview. You can even use a stack of books. What you don't want to do is hold the phone for the duration of the interview; this is a professional encounter, not a FaceTime chat with your grandma.

Like any interview, make sure you have studied up on the company and position you wish to hold. Google them. See if they have had any news lately. Did they recently merge with anyone? Or perhaps they made a branding change not long ago. In the very least, know the goods and/or services they offer, and be prepared to tell them how you could aid them in this niche if you were hired.

Prepare questions. Almost always the interviewer will ask you if you have any questions, and if they have answered all of them, its fine to tell them so. However, this is your chance to have their undivided attention, and ESPECIALLY if you are offered a job directly following. You will want to have compiled a list of anything you might have wanted to know, rather than bombarding the interviewer's inbox with emails less than 24 hours after they had time set aside to make themselves available just for you.

With these tips you will be well on your way to not only acing that interview, but job offers galore! Break a leg and most of all, be yourself, and let your personality shine!

Co-Author Colette Pfeiffer Talent Booking Experts & Connections Consulting and Marketing Solutions team.

PHOTO BY POLINA ZIMMERMAN

New

NEW & NOTEWORTHY

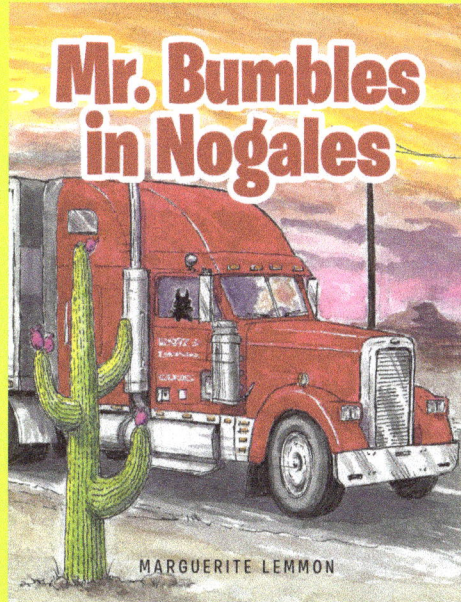

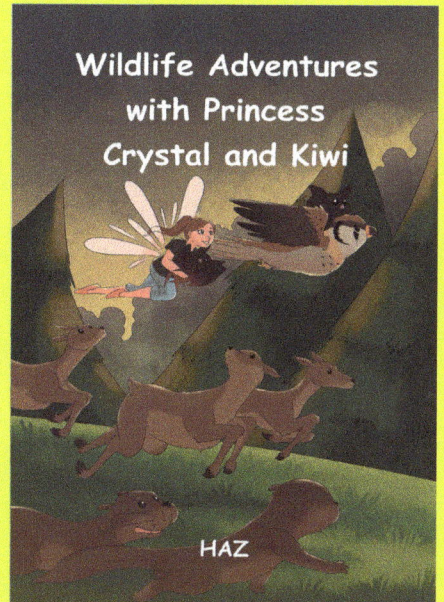

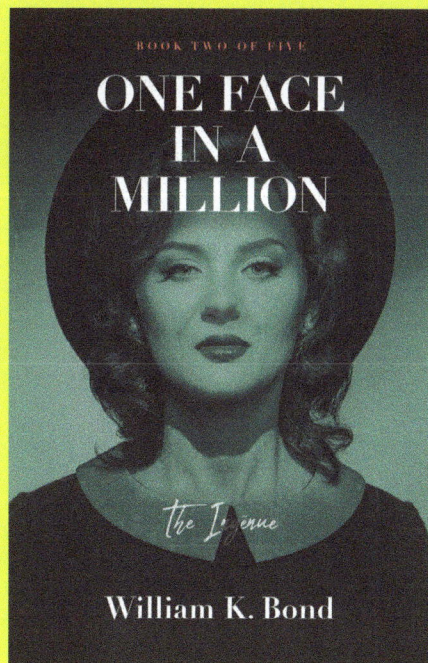

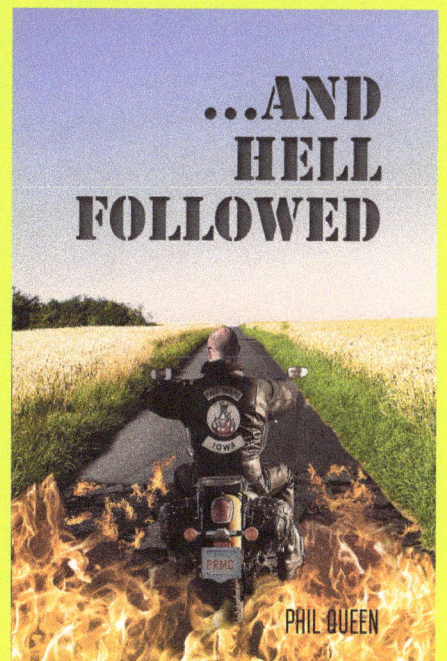

Mr. Bumbles in Nogales
MARGUERITE LEMMON

Wildlife Adventures with Princess Crystal and Kiwi
HAZ

BOOK TWO OF FIVE
ONE FACE IN A MILLION
The Ingenue
William K. Bond

...AND HELL FOLLOWED
PHIL QUEEN

Avaiable at bookstores everywhere, or online at the Apple iBooks Store, Amazon, or Barnes & Noble.

BOOK

Health

Are You S***ting Me?! How to Survive, Thrive and Transform Through Colorectal Cancer, written by Oils & Spoils blogger Kim Mullins, is available for pre-order through 1 a.m., April 22. Are You S***ting Me?! is an irreverent, yet informational play-by-play of how to navigate, understand and plan for surviving, thriving and transforming through illness.

Author of Are You S***ting Me?! How to Survive, Thrive and Transform Through Colorectal Cancer

Health

Personal Experience of Colorectal Cancer is an Irreverent, Cheeky Tail of Surviving, Thriving and Transforming Through Illness

Are You S***ting Me?! How to Survive, Thrive and Transform Through Colorectal Cancer, written by Oils & Spoils blogger Kim Mullins, is available for pre-order through 1 a.m., April 22. Are You S***ting Me?! is an irreverent, yet informational play-by-play of how to navigate, understand and plan for surviving, thriving and transforming through illness.

"Personal experiences of colorectal cancer are few and far between, and the subject itself seems more taboo than talking about sex. Not that cancer is sexy, butt seriously, we need to talk about it. See what I did there?" the book's author, Kim Harris Mullins, said.

In the United States, colorectal cancer cases are on the rise, and the larges demographic for this recent uptick are millennials. According to the American Cancer Society:

Millennials born around 1990 are two times more likely to develop colon cancer and four times more likely to develop rectal cancer compared to young adults in the 1950s.
The rate of colorectal cancer has

been steadily increasing among adults younger than 50 since the mid-1980s. Conversely, incidences of colorectal cancers have dropped for those over age 50. Young adults are more likely to be diagnosed with a late stage of colorectal cancer due to the perception by both young adults and doctors that they are not likely to develop the disease.
Deaths from colorectal cancer for people younger than age 55 have increased 2 percent every year from 2007 to 2016.
Colorectal cancer is the third leading cause of cancer-related deaths in men and women.
Colorectal cancer is the second most common cause of cancer-related deaths in men and women combined.
The lifetime risk for developing colorectal cancer is 1 in 23 for men and 1 in 25 for women.
The number of new colorectal cancer cases estimated for 2020 is 147,950.
104,610 new cases of colon cancer
43,340 new cases of rectal cancer
Regardless of the "type" of cancer you might have, this book promotes:

Awareness of the rise of colorectal cancer and what you can do

for prevention
The importance of early screening
How to advocate for your own health before, during, and after cancer Unique organizational tools to help you through your journey Reframing your brain and other coping techniques
Thriving after cancer, including living with an ostomy and paying it forward A s***load of funny anecdotes (hey, humor helps, right?)

"During my cancer journey, I went through radiation, chemo, and surgery, which resulted in a permanent colostomy bag, post-op chemo, and external lupus caused by the chemo. Don't even get me started on jokes around being a 'bag' lady," Mullins said. "Having cancer was the scariest time of my life, and I wish I'd had someone to talk to openly about what I was experiencing.

Are You S***ting Me?! is the inspirational, informational, but oh-so-hilarious guide I wish I'd had before, during, and after my struggle."

New

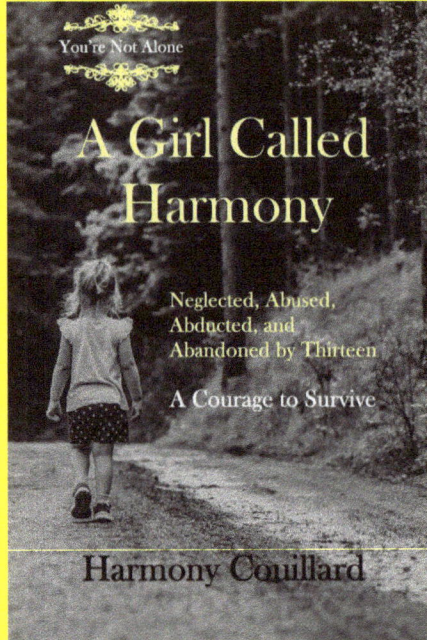

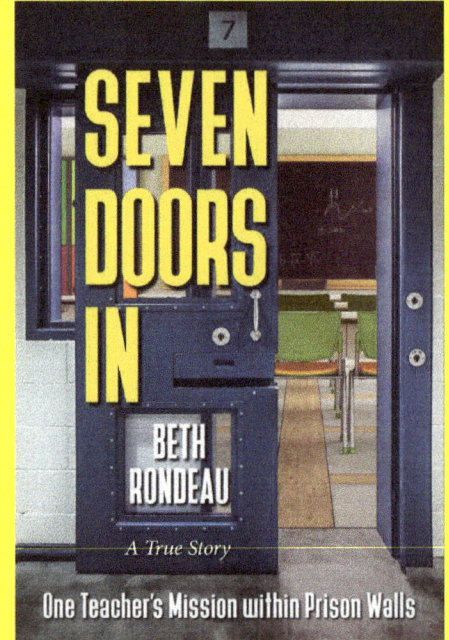

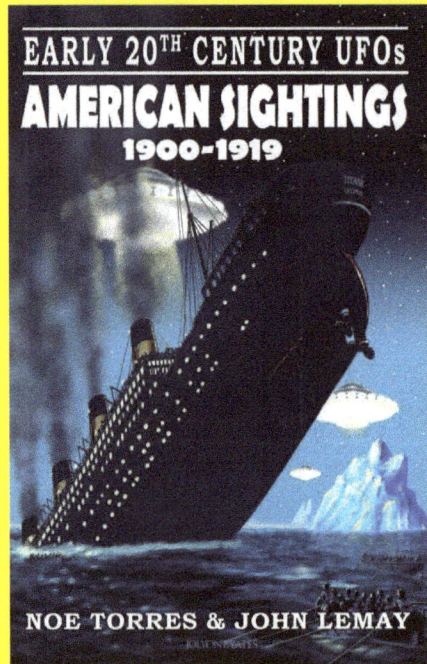

New

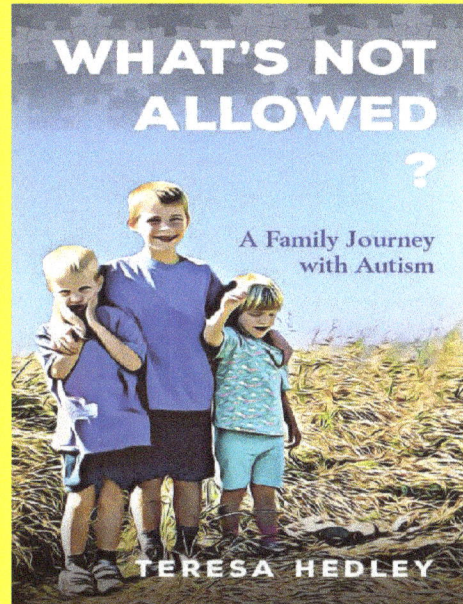

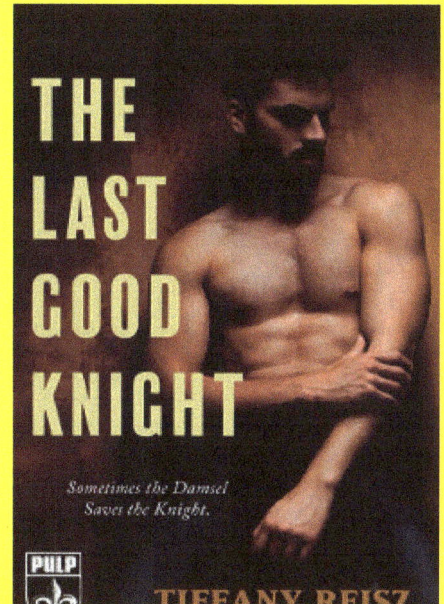

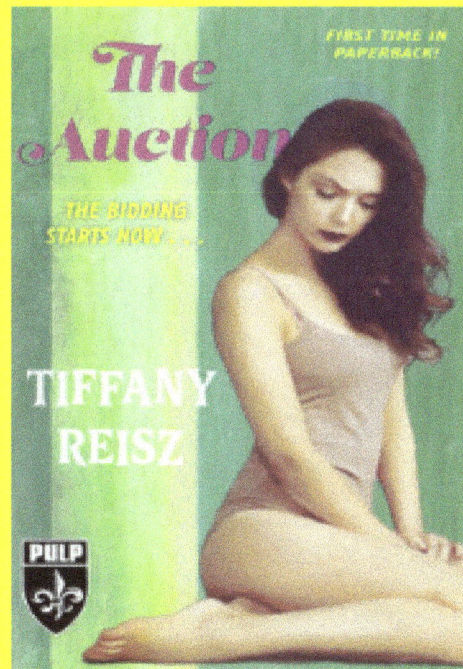

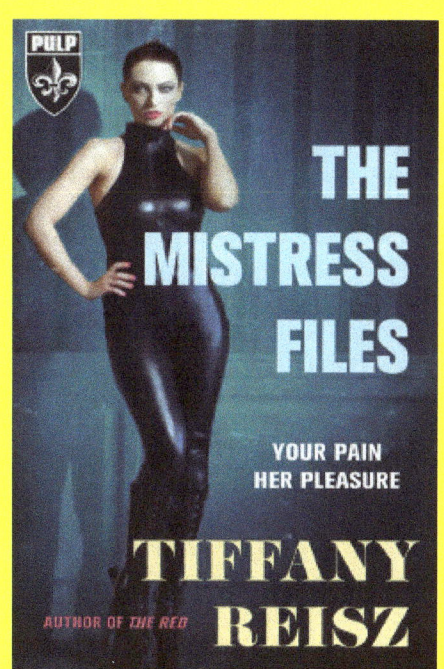

DOES ASTROLOGY REALLY WORK?

If you ask hardened scientists, they will say astrology can't work. On the other hand, believers will give the opposite opinion. And the truth is that both are right. Actually, it all depends upon the definition of "work". Basically, astrology refers to the belief that the stars and planets have an impact on a person's environment, personality, and mood based on when that person was born. Let's find out more.

You may have seen horoscopes published in newspapers. They are given by birth dates, and make predictions about people's lives and personalities. Besides, they give them advice based on the position of the astronomical bodies.

According to a survey done by the National Science Foundation, 41% respondents were of the opinion that astrology is kind of scientific.

The Position of Astronomical Bodies

The orientation and position of the sun in relation to Earth create seasons. We know that solar flares create electromagnetic disturbances on our planet. This process can cause blackouts and satellite disruptions. Besides, the moon position creates ocean tides. For instance, if you are a fisherman, the moon position can have an impact on your livelihood. On the other hand, the solar wind creates fascinating aura. And the biggest fact is that sunlight is the only biggest source of energy for us all.

Can Horoscopes make you Feel Better?

The short answer is, yes. The thing is that horoscopes can make you feel better. This is partly because of the placebo effect, which is a psychological effect. Basically, this effect happens when believing in a strange method makes you feel better. Actually, it's the belief that makes you feel better, not the method. According to scientists, the placebo effect is proven. For instance, if you give tablets containing plain water to 10 patients and tell them the tablets can help them get better much sooner, many of the patients will get better. It's because of the placebo effect. The new drug must perform much better than the placebo effect. In the experiment conducted by experts, the control group involved patients that received a placebo effect. Actually, this is the mechanism that makes astrology work for people.

You will find a lot of people who believe in astrology. They feel better when they follow the advice given in horoscopes. The same is true about a lot of pseudo-scientific treatments including homeopathy and crystal healing.

Actually, a new medicine shouldn't be proven to help patients feel better. There should be a proof that it works beyond the placebo effect. This is what we need to build a strong case.

If you stick to a scientifically proven treatment, you will have a belief that the treatment will work for you. For instance, you should go for a walk instead of reading horoscope in a newspaper. We know that exercise helps improve your mental and physical health.

Long story short, if you are into astrology, we suggest that you read this article again and review your understanding about horoscopy. Hopefully, you will find this article greatly helpful.

BY DHANUSUYA K

SOURCE: EzineArticles

BOOK REVIEW

Harbor's Edge by Sanne Rothman

BY LISA BROWN GILBERT

Follow the F.B.I. Criminal Profiling rules. Dig up secrets on a Hawaiian island. Accept that sometimes only evil can push you to love. Harbor has lost too much already, yet finds herself in a race to uncover clues that unlock a strange mystery linked not only to her dad's murder but to an ancient legend that links us all. Author Sanne Rothman presents the 1st novel featuring The Untold Legend of the MO'O, a shape-shifting water lizard that steals your soul right before your eyes…unless the heart is stolen first.

Sanne Rothman's young adult thriller, Harbor's Edge, piques the curiosity while romancing the imagination, with a story that offers mystery, the supernatural, budding romance, and an intelligent 14-year-old heroine on a profoundly insightful journey to self-discovery. The story is set in beautiful Hawaii with which author Sanne Rothman does a wonderful job of detailing the beautiful environment. She brings forth both its timeless natural beauty as well as artfully presents intriguing aspects of Hawaiian life and culture especially with her incorporation of the lore of the dark and ancient sea monsters called The Mo'o, the legend, and mystery of which is initially contemplated by Harbor early on in the story. Initially, as the story unfolds, we meet Harbor, a young, resilient, intelligent teenager who finds her life shrouded in mystery and sadness. Having lost both her parents under mysterious circumstances, she fights with feelings of abandonment as she seeks to solve the mystery of what truly happened. She lost her F.B.I. agent father to a cold-blooded murderer and her mother, who disappeared without a trace, leaving her and her younger sister Fig in the care of their TuTu (grandmother). TuTu owns a popular, local restaurant, featuring Hawaiian hamburgers and Harbor works at the restaurant in the drive-through which allows her the opportunity to practice analyzing the faces of customers based

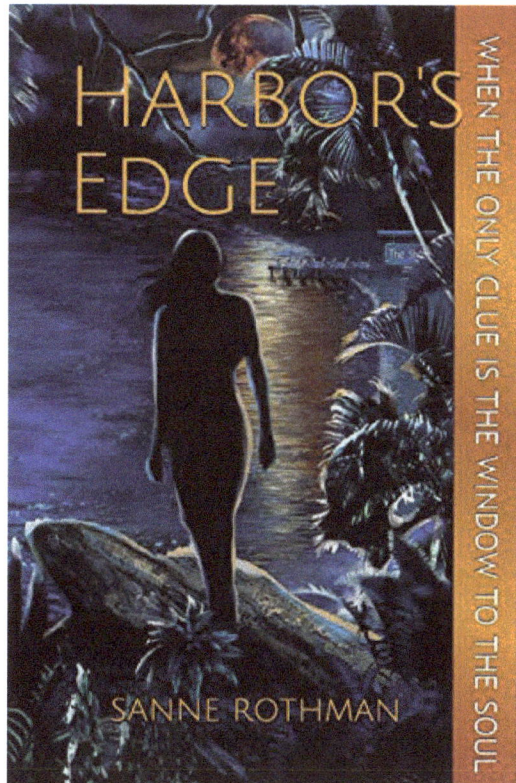

on techniques from her father's FBI profiling manuals. She works on her skills at analyzing faces in the hopes of finding clues to her father's murderer and clues to her missing mother.

Overall a story filled with well-plotted twists and turns fueled by excitement and building tensions when children begin to turn up missing and Harbor thinks she may have a lead. Moreover, the story carries a mystery within a mystery as Harbor makes a friend at school, Keyne, with whom the sparks of first love begin to ignite, however, he seems to have an air of secrecy surrounding him as well.

Altogether, Harbor's Edge turned out to be both an imaginative and absorbing read that I thoroughly

enjoyed. I found myself instantly drawn into the beautifully set world of Harbor, shrouded in mystery, supernatural legacy, and artfully fueled with intriguing plot twists including, the unique inclusion of clues disbursed within each chapter. Additionally, I also enjoyed the likable characters within the story, especially that of Harbor. She's a relatable and intelligent character, easy to sympathize with and whose exciting journey to self-discovery was easy to follow. Absolutely, a worthwhile and noteworthy read that left me wanting more. I look forward to Book 2, Keyne, and The Wrath of The Mo'o. Overall, this would make a good choice for an end of summer read and I recommend it.
Source: EzineArticles

www.ingramcontent.com/pod-product-compliance
Lightning Source LLC
Chambersburg PA
CBHW052348210326
41597CB00037B/6299